Most copperheads have copper-colored heads and hourglass-shaped brown bands along their bodies. The colors vary among the subspecies. The southern copperhead has a pink-colored head, while the northern copperhead has a red-colored head. The color of these snakes' bodies also varies. They can be a light shade of pink or tan or a darker reddish-brown.

A snake's bands can help people identify its subspecies. Each variety has a different band thickness and pattern. The northern copperhead is the only species with small dark spots on its sides between the bands. All of these patterns and colors help copperheads blend

Close Cousins

Copperheads are closely related to another pit viper, the cottonmouth. This snake is also known as the water moccasin. It lives in freshwater areas. Cottonmouths share many similar characteristics and behaviors with copperheads. This includes the hourglass-shaped bands along their bodies. As cottonmouths grow and get older, however, the bands become darker until they disappear.

in with their surroundings. This allows them to hide and watch for prey.

Built to Seek

Copperheads have a good sense of smell, but they do not use their nostrils. They use their tongues to smell instead! Like other snakes, copperheads only use their nostrils for breathing. But by flicking their forked tongues, copperheads are able to gather scent particles from the ground and the air. Their tongues help them sniff out their next meal and any predators.

Copperheads also have good eyesight. This is because of their elliptical pupils. While many animals have round pupils, a copperhead's are long and thin. This provides them with excellent night vision.

Copperheads do not have ears. They cannot hear sounds the same way humans do. Instead they sense vibrations on the ground or in the air. This helps them gather information about their surroundings.

Copperheads use their tongues to find potential mates during breeding season.

Copperheads use all of these senses as they search for food. And they need them. From the moment they are born, copperheads have to survive on their own.

CHAPTER TWO

All in the Family

Copperheads mate in late spring or early fall. Male copperheads start looking for a mate when they are approximately four years old. They will have grown to be approximately two feet (1 m) long. Female copperheads are ready to mate at approximately three years old. Usually only the largest and oldest females breed.

Males sometimes travel long distances in search of a female mate.

Chasing a Female

A male copperhead has a special way of getting a female. He starts by moving his chin across the ground. If the female moves away, he follows her. He tries to put his head on some part of her body. The female responds by waving her tail in the air. She moves it back and forth slowly, whips it around quickly, or shakes it rapidly. He continues to rub his head on her head until she accepts him.

Mating

When a male finds a suitable female, he will most likely have to fight for her. These battles are not fierce. The two males face each other and raise their upper bodies off of the ground. Then they try to push each other down. The snake that is the first to pin down its opponent's head is the winner. Neither snake is hurt, but the copperhead that loses will probably never try to win a female again.

Sometimes females copy this behavior to find a strong mate. When a male approaches a female, she may raise herself up as if she wants to fight.

If a male backs away when a female raises herself to fight, she will not mate with him.

An Unusual Nursery

After copperheads mate, the male and female go their separate ways. The female carries the babies for approximately 105 to 110 days. During this time, she moves to what is called a birthing rookery. This is often a log or a rock pile. The rookery provides shelter and safety from predators, such as owls and hawks. There she may meet with other female copperheads. They share the rookery until their young are born. This usually occurs in late summer.

Copperheads are born alive and must quickly learn to take care of themselves.

Copperheads are ovoviviparous. This means the babies develop in an egg inside the female. A young snake receives nourishment from its egg's yolk. The egg eventually hatches inside the female. When it is time, the babies are born alive. Only a thin membrane surrounds them when they are born. After the young snakes break out of their membranes, their mother does not take care of them at all.

Female copperheads can give birth to between two and seventeen babies. It is most common for them to have between six and nine babies. Larger females tend to have more young. Newborn copperheads weigh less than one-half of an ounce (14 g) each. They range in length from 8 to 10 inches (20 to 25 cm).

Baby copperheads look similar to adults. They are born with fangs and venom. But unlike adults, newborns have bright yellow tails. When young copperheads wriggle or twist, their tails look similar to little worms. Hungry frogs and lizards

Growing New Skin

A copperhead's skin does not grow. But the copperhead still does! As it grows, its skin becomes too tight. The snake must then shed it. It gets rid of the old skin by rubbing itself on a rough surface such as a rock or a tree. There is already new, better-fitting skin underneath. Copperheads start this process early. They first shed their skin a few days after birth. Their eyes get cloudy for some of the time they are shedding. This makes them vulnerable to attack.

Copperheads' bodies slow down and require little energy during the cold months.

come to investigate, and the young snakes catch their first prey.

Cold Weather

As cold weather sets in, young copperheads move into an underground den. Although they do not truly hibernate, they stay in the den all winter long.

Life Span

Among the different subspecies, most wild copperheads live between one and seven years. Some copperheads in captivity live to be 18 years old. One northern copperhead in captivity was recorded as being almost 30 years old.

EXPLORE ONLINE

The focus of Chapter Two is the copperhead life cycle. It also touches on the appearance of newborn copperheads. The website below focuses on venomous snakes and their nonvenomous look-alikes, including baby copperheads. As you know, every source is different. How is the information given on the website different from the information in this chapter? What information is the same? How do the two sources present information differently?

Copperhead Snakes
www.mycorelibrary.com/copperheads

CHAPTER THREE

On the Move . . . or Not

Copperheads are not the fastest snakes. They are sometimes thought of as being lethargic, or slow and lazy. But there are certain times when copperheads move quickly.

Copperheads are cold-blooded. Their body temperature changes with the temperature of their environment. Copperheads are most active at dawn and dusk during the warmer months between March

Copperheads rely on camouflage to hide from predators since they are not the fastest snakes.

and late October. But they do avoid getting too hot. They become more active at night to avoid overheating. In spring and autumn, when the weather is cooler, they move around during the day.

A warm, humid night after a rainfall is a good time to be a copperhead. The temperature is warm enough to be active, but not too hot to move. The wet ground makes it easier to smell and follow prey. The darkness provides protection from predators such as owls, opossums, and raccoons.

A Full Menu

Copperheads sometimes travel up to two miles (3 km) to find food or a mate. Though

Cicadas for Dinner

It is easy to imagine copperheads eating mice. But what about copperheads feasting on cicadas? That is what happened in 1949. On the banks of the Colorado River, cicadas came up from the ground and into the oak trees. Normally a ground snake, copperheads crawled along the wild grapevines that grew around the trunks. Dozens of copperheads were seen stretched out or coiled up on the branches. The snakes stuffed themselves with cicadas.

Mice are one of the many animals that copperheads eat.

most of their diet is made up of rodents, copperheads are opportunistic feeders. This means they eat what is available. Copperheads have been known to eat more than 30 different types of prey. Meals can include insects, lizards, frogs, salamanders, small snakes, birds, and small mammals. Some large copperheads have even been known to eat small box turtles.

As Still as a Statue

Like other pit vipers, the copperhead is mostly an ambush predator. It finds a good location, takes its position, and waits for prey to arrive. Hidden among fallen leaves, it can remain motionless for hours or even days.

Copperheads sometimes seek out their prey. Copperheads move so slowly and smoothly that they do not make a sound. It is hard for their prey to detect them.

When unsuspecting prey is close enough, a copperhead will grab it. If the prey is small, the snake holds it in its mouth until it stops struggling. Then it swallows the animal headfirst. If the prey is a larger animal, the copperhead first strikes the prey. It bites with its fangs and injects the animal with venom. The snake then backs away and waits. If it ate the animal right away, the copperhead could be injured as the animal struggled. The prey wanders off. But because

The snake follows its prey using its heat-sensing pits and forked tongue.

of the venom, it does not get far. Once the animal has died, the copperhead can safely eat it.

A copperhead can survive on only eight to twelve meals between May and late October. Copperheads do not eat at all during the winter months. Though

Better than Dracula's

A copperhead relies on its fangs to catch its prey. These fangs are secured to the snake's upper jawbone. When the copperhead opens its mouth, the fangs come down. When the snake closes its mouth again, the fangs fold back up against the roof of its mouth. Sometimes a copperhead will lose a fang. But with five to seven fully grown replacement fangs, a new one is ready to fill the spot.

they are inactive in cold weather, they do not truly hibernate. They spend the winter in dens, often near the top of a rocky ridge. Sometimes they share the den with other copperheads or even other species of snakes. They usually use the same den year after year.

Venom from the southern copperhead contains a protein that may help fight cancer. But collecting enough snake venom for testing isn't easy. Frank Markland, a professor at the University of Southern California, explains:

> The problem with a snake-venom derived protein is that you'd have to milk every copperhead in existence to get enough to treat one patient. This just doesn't provide enough protein in terms of our long-term goals of clinical trials. As a solution, one of our researchers developed a method to engineer the genetic material that codes for this protein in bacteria. So now, we can grow these bacteria in large vats to make a new protein . . . which mimics the activity of the snake venom protein.

> Source: "Using Snake Venom Protein to Fight Cancer." American Museum of Natural History. *American Museum of Natural History*, March 1, 2012. Web. Accessed January 24, 2014.

Consider Your Audience

Read this passage by Frank Markland closely. How might you explain it differently to your science teacher, your friends, or a younger sibling? Write a letter to one of them, describing what you learned.

CHAPTER FOUR

Home Sweet Home

Copperheads are found throughout the eastern and central United States. Northern and southern copperheads live east of the Mississippi River. Trans-Pecos, Osage, and broad-banded copperheads are found west of the Mississippi River. Of the five subspecies, the northern copperhead has the largest range. It lives in northern Georgia and Alabama, as far north as Massachusetts,

Southern copperheads live in the southeastern United States.

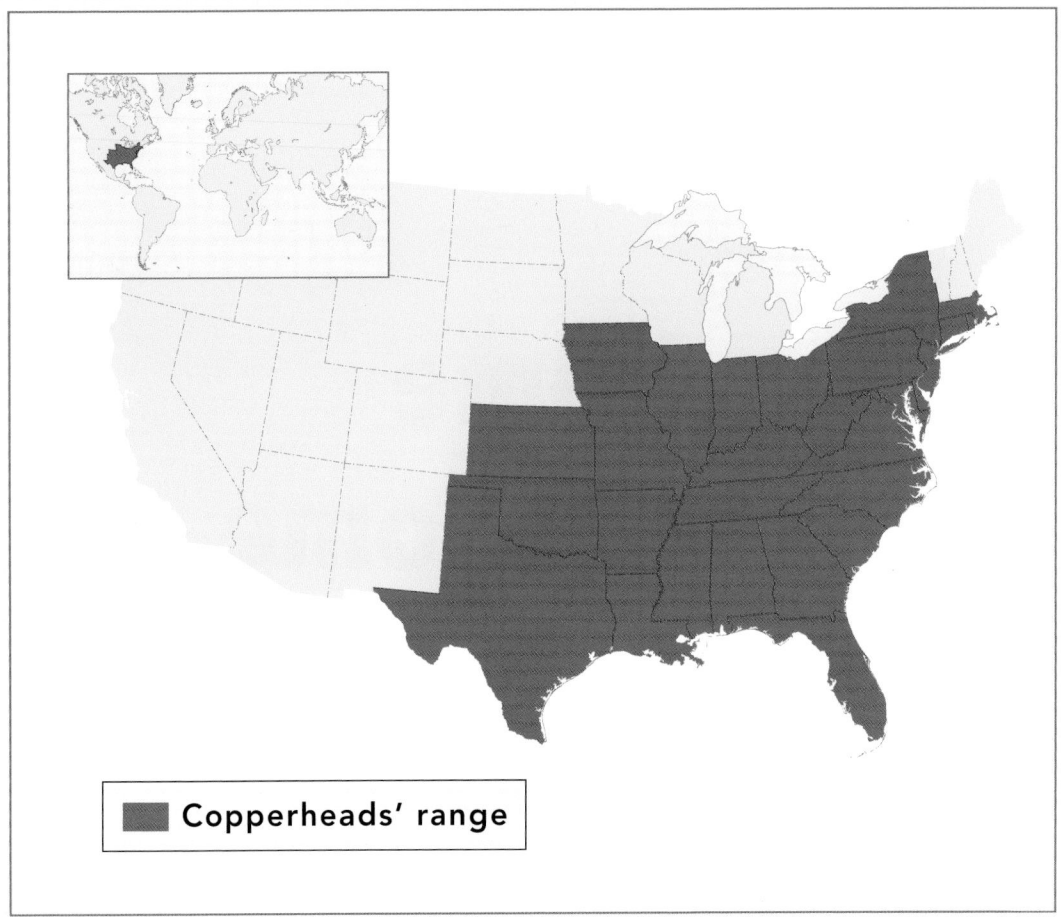

Copperheads in the United States

Look at this map of the United States. Notice all the states where copperheads can be found. How does this information compare with what you learned from the text? Based on where you live, will you be more watchful for copperheads the next time you are outside?

and as far west as Illinois. Some copperhead species can also be found in parts of Mexico. Copperheads can be found in areas with suitable prey.

Country Snakes

Copperheads are at home in a variety of habitats. Northern copperheads live on dry, rocky hillsides and wooded parts of mountains. They use rocky slopes for cover. They also hide in holes. Copperheads need to bask in the sun. The sun gives them energy. They often rest on rocky ledges. Southern copperheads prefer wooded areas near ponds and streams. Fallen leaves, underbrush, hay fields, meadows, orchards, and canyons make for good copperhead homes.

No Relation

The Australian common copperhead is similar to the copperheads of North America. The Australian snake is also poisonous. Its bite is also rarely fatal. And these copperheads generally try to avoid humans. But the Australian copperhead is in a whole different family. It is not a pit viper. It is found in cooler climates around dams, canals, and even drainage ditches. When threatened, it flattens its head and thrashes its body. But it is slow to bite.

City Snakes

Copperheads also feel at home among human-made structures. They are seen around abandoned farms and junkyards. Broken foundations, wooden structures, and old cellars also make good copperhead habitats. Construction rubble, sawdust, and woodpiles are good homes for them too. Although it is rare, copperheads sometimes live in cities, in areas near parks or woodlots.

Social Snakes

Copperheads stay close to each other while sunning, courting, mating, eating, and drinking. Other copperheads, black rat snakes, and timber

Copperheads in Captivity

Believe it or not, some people keep copperheads as pets. It takes a very experienced snake handler to keep one safely. Not only does the cage need to be escape-proof, but it also must be in an escape-proof room. Even with many precautions, snake owners still sometimes get bitten. That is why some states have made it illegal to keep copperheads or other venomous snakes as pets.

Copperheads are social snakes and do not mind company.

Copperheads do not usually wander far from their home except to search for a mate.

rattlesnakes can be found sharing the same dens for the winter.

Once a copperhead has found a home, it will usually stay year-round. For one study, scientists marked and released several adult copperheads. They found them one year later. All of the copperheads were within 100 yards (91 m) of the release site.

There are several myths about copperheads. The Brown Family Environmental Center at Kenyon College explained the myth of pilot snakes in their winter 2012 newsletter:

> *Black Rat Snakes are also sometimes referred to as 'Pilot Snakes,' based on the notion that they lead Copperheads to safety, and if a Rat Snake is spotted, you can be sure there is a Copperhead lurking behind it. . . .*
>
> *Some of these stories do contain a microscopic bit of truth . . . Copperheads, Rattlesnakes, and Black Rat Snakes all hibernate in similar areas, often a deep rocky crevice on a sunny slope. During Ohio's settlement in the early 19th century, settlers often found these and other snakes seemingly 'living' together in these areas, and somewhere the myth of the 'Pilot Snake' was born.*

Source: "Copperheads Fact & Fiction." Brown Family Environmental Center at Kenyon College. Kenyon College, 2012. Web. Accessed January 24, 2014.

What's the Big Idea?

What is the main idea behind this article about black rat snakes and copperheads? Are there other myths about copperheads that people believe? Do these also support the main idea of this article? Why or why not?

Endangered?

As venomous reptiles, copperheads are near the top of the food chain. They do have some natural enemies, though. Hawks and owls sometimes eat copperheads. Raccoons, opossums, and king snakes will eat them too. But the biggest threat to copperheads comes from humans.

Copperheads do not have many natural predators, but they are threatened by human activity.

A copperhead may first give a warning bite to whatever is threatening it. The snake will let out a small amount of venom.

No Warning

Many pit vipers have a warning system they use when they are cornered. For instance, a rattlesnake holds a defensive pose and shakes the rattle at the end of its tail. It may attack if startled, but it can only strike from a coiled position. A cottonmouth will vibrate its tail and open its white mouth to flash a warning. Some copperheads vibrate their tails rapidly, but they do not have rattles. The snake must be among dry leaves for the tail to make a sound and sound like a rattle. Or the copperhead may give off an unpleasant smell. But for the most part, copperheads simply strike without an obvious warning.

Fearful Reactions

People often kill copperheads because they are afraid of being bitten. Yet copperheads are generally not aggressive. Most bites occur when people threaten the snakes. Sometimes copperheads even use a warning bite. These dry bites inject a small amount of venom or even none at all. At least 25 percent of all copperhead bites do not involve venom.

People also harm copperheads in other

Snakebite First Aid

Copperhead bites should be taken seriously. If bitten by one of these snakes, stay calm and get away from the snake. Do not try to catch or kill it. Check for symptoms of poisoning. These include intense, burning pain and swelling in the bite area. Do not apply ice or cold. Get medical help right away, even if you do not have any symptoms of poisoning.

Copperheads are an important part of the ecosystem. It is important for humans to continue protecting these snakes' habitats.

ways. Some people kill them just because they are poisonous. Sometimes cars hit snakes that are crossing roads. Many times, copperhead habitats are destroyed by human activities, such as building new roads, businesses, and homes. Without a home, many copperheads die or are forced to move. New habitats

FURTHER EVIDENCE

Chapter Five discusses the dangers copperheads encounter. What was one of the chapter's main points about predators? What are some pieces of evidence that support this main point? Read the article on the website at the link below. Find a quote from the website to support this point. Does the quote support an existing piece of evidence or add a new one?

Copperhead Threats
www.mycorelibrary.com/copperheads

may not be safe for them. Pollution created by human activities can also harm these snakes.

Copperheads do not have endangered or threatened status. It is important they stay that way. Copperheads play an important role in the ecosystem by controlling rodent populations. Without snakes like these, some habitats would be overrun with rodents. Rodents would damage crops and spread diseases. By understanding copperheads, we can learn how to share our world with them.

Common Name: Copperhead

Scientific Name: *Agkistrodon contortrix*

Average Size: 24 to 36 inches (61 to 91 cm)

Average Weight: Less than one pound (0.5 kg)

Color: Tan, pink, or reddish-brown with dark brown hourglass-shaped bands

Average Life Span: Up to 18 years in the wild

Diet: Insects, lizards, frogs, salamanders, small snakes, birds, and rodents

Habitat: Rocky hillsides, wooded mountain areas, wooded areas near ponds and streams, sawdust piles, abandoned buildings, and stone walls

Predators: Humans, owls, hawks, opossums, raccoons, wild pigs, and king snakes

Did You Know?

- The longer a copperhead is, the longer its fangs are.
- The yellow tip on a copperhead's tail fades as the snake gets older. It is usually gone by age three or four.
- Copperheads have hinged jaws that allow them to swallow larger prey whole.
- Copperheads bite more people in the United States than any other venomous snake.

Say What?

Studying copperheads can mean learning a lot of new vocabulary. Find five words in this book you've never heard or seen before. Use a dictionary to find out what they mean. Using your own ideas, write down the meaning of each word. Then write a sentence using each word.

Another View

There are many different sources of information about copperheads. As you know, every source is different. Ask a librarian or another adult to help you find a reliable source about these snakes. Write a short essay comparing and contrasting the new source's point of view with the ideas in this book. How are the sources similar? How are the sources different? Why do you think they are similar or different?

Why Do I Care?

Chapter Four discusses where copperheads live. Even if you don't live in one of those areas, why should you still care about copperheads? Write down two or three reasons humans should care about copperhead populations.

Surprise Me

Learning about copperheads can be interesting and surprising. Think about what you learned from this book. Can you name two or three facts about copperheads you found surprising? Why did you find this information surprising?

GLOSSARY

birthing rookery
a place where a group of animals gives birth

camouflage
patterns or coloring that help disguise or hide an animal

cicada
a stout-bodied insect with a wide head and transparent wings that makes a loud buzzing noise

hibernate
to pass the winter in a sleeping state

lethargic
slow or lazy

membrane
a soft, flexible covering

opportunistic
taking advantage of opportunities as they arise

ovoviviparous
producing young by means of eggs that are hatched within the body of the parent

predator
an animal that kills and eats other animals

prey
an animal hunted or killed by another animal for food

rodent
a small mammal that has sharp front teeth for gnawing

subspecies
a classification category just below species

LEARN MORE

Books

Gunderson, Megan M. *Copperheads*. Minneapolis, Abdo Publishing, 2011.

Kalman, Bobbie. *The Life Cycle of a Snake*. New York: Crabtree Publishing, 2003.

Shupe, Scott. *US Guide to Venomous Snakes and Their Mimics*. New York: Skyhorse Publishing, 2011.

Websites

To learn more about Amazing Reptiles, visit **booklinks.abdopublishing.com**. These links are routinely monitored and updated to provide the most current information available.

Visit **www.mycorelibrary.com** for free additional tools for teachers and students.

INDEX

ABOUT THE AUTHOR

Samantha Bell has written and/or illustrated more than 20 books for children. She loves learning about nature and wildlife—there are so many incredible creatures out there!